Werewolf HAIKU

Ryan Mecum

HOW BOOKS

Cincinnati, Ohio

www.howdesign.com

Published by HOW Books, an imprint of F+W Media, Inc., 4700
East Galbraith Road, Cincinnati, Ohio 45236. (800) 289-0963.
First edition.

For more excellent books and resources for designers, visit
www.howdesign.com.

14 13 12 11 10   5 4 3 2 1

Distributed in Canada by Fraser Direct, 100 Armstrong Avenue,
Georgetown, Ontario, Canada L7G 5S4, Tel: (905) 877-4411.
Distributed in the U.K. and Europe by David & Charles, Brunel
House, Newton Abbot, Devon, TQ12 4PU, England, Tel: (+44)
1626-323200, Fax: (+44) 1626-323319, E-mail: postmaster@
davidandcharles.co.uk. Distributed in Australia by Capricorn
Link, P.O. Box 704, Windsor, NSW 2756 Australia, Tel: (02)
4577-3555.

Library of Congress Cataloging-in-Publication Data
Mecum, Ryan.
    Werewolf haiku / Ryan Mecum.
        p. cm.
    ISBN 978-1-4403-0826-0 (pbk. : alk. paper)
1. Haiku--Humor. 2. Werewolves--Humor. 3. Werewolves--
Poetry. I. Title.
    PN6231.H28M428 2010
    818'.602--dc22
                    2010012988

Editor: Amy Schell Owen
HOW Books Art Director: Grace Ring
Production Coordinator: Greg Nock

Designer/Packager:
Lisa Kuhn, Curio Press, LLC
www.curiopress.com

This journal belongs to

_____

REQUESTED

3609

NOTICE

S0000019278108

Dear haiku journal:
This could be my last entry
if I have rabies.

A stray dog bit me
while I delivered the mail.
Should have used the mace.

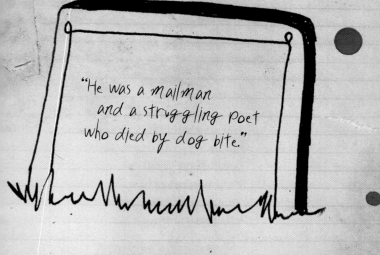

"He was a mailman
and a struggling poet
who died by dog bite."

The dog seemed homeless.
It looked like a rabid wolf,
   hungry for mailmen.

I kicked and he ran—
   but not before he bit off
   a big chunk of calf.

2

I finished the route,
hobbling to each mailbox,
and thinking of Rose.

Rose is my lady,
but she might not know it yet
since we're yet to speak.

I'm introverted
and I would guess she is, too,
judging by her mail.

We differ in ways.
She subscribes to Cat Fancy.
I get Dog Fancy.

I limp through her yard
and as I fill her mailbox,
she opens her door.

With her lovely smile,
Rose greets me with a hello.
I nod back and leave.

I've always been shy,
which is why I don't respond
and why I'm alone.

4

I like to pretend
I will ask Rose out someday,
since I won't for real.

5

Y STALKER LOVE SONG MIX!

1. Blondie - One Way or Another
2. The Police - Can't Stand Losing You
3. Cheap Trick - I Want You To Want Me
4. U2 - I Will Follow
5. Backstreet Boys - As Long As You Love Me
6. David Seville - Witch Doctor
7. Screaming Jay Hawkings - I Put a Spell on You
8. The Stranglers - In the Shadows
9. Darren Hayes - Creepin' Up on You
10. Diana Ross - I'm Gonna Make You Love Me
11. Duran Duran - Hungry Like the Wolf
12. Sarah McLachlan - Possession
13. Fleetwood Mac - Say You Love Me
14. Death Cab For Cutie - I Will Possess Your Heart
15. The Police - Every Breath You Take
16. Morrissey - The More You Ignore Me, The Closer I Get
17. Meatloaf - I'd Do Anything For Love (But I Won't Do That)
18. Michael Bolton - How Am I Supposed to Live Without You
19. Billy Ocean - Get Outta My Dreams, Get Into My Car
20. Bryan Adams - (Everything I Do) I Do It For You
21. Elvis Costello - I Want You

6

When I get back home,
    I play my love mix CD,
    write haiku and cry.

    What a rotten day!
I dodge the girl of my dreams
and I'm still bleeding.

Lupé my Shih Tzu
sniffs at my gouged-out calf wound
and whimpers away.

The cut oozes pus
and my whole sock is dark red
from blood draining down.

All around the wound
are many long strands of hair...
which are not from me.

8

Rubbing alcohol
burns as I clean out the cut,
visibly throbbing.

I'll wrap my dog bite,
fall asleep on the front couch,
and dream about Rose.

That's it for now, friend.
I'll write in you tomorrow,
dear haiku journal.

9

Dear haiku journal,
I think I killed some people.
That was no dog bite.

What happened last night?
My selective memory
is a bit hazy.

It wasn't a dream,
due to my lack of clothing,
and I'm really full.

I woke up naked,
sprawled in a stranger's front yard.
Rough start to a day.

You hate alarm clocks?
Try automatic sprinklers
with you in grass, nude.

"Looks like you woke up
on the wrong side of the bed"
should now be retired.

From now on, I'll say,
"Looks like somebody woke up
outside, nude and wet."

11

My mind starts to fill
with memories of chaos
and eating neighbors.

The woman next door
with that huge mole on her neck—
I think I ate it.

It's an odd feeling
when realization hits—
that now I murder.

12

Sprinting to my house,
   while covering my privates,
  through suburbia.

Kids at their bus stop
  are not sure how to react
as I run past them.

"Bus driver, guess what?
We just saw some naked dude,
   covered all in blood!"

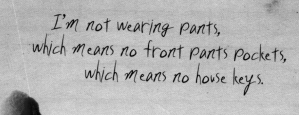

I'm not wearing pants,
which means no front pants pockets,
which means no house keys.

Banging on my door,
knowing only I live there,
hoping I answer.

The "Three Pigs" story—
a wolf screaming, "Let me in!"
seems applicable.

14

I check the back door,
which I recall kicking down
when I left last night.

I run in my house
and go straight to a mirror
to see who I am.

I stare back at me,
  but I remember the face
  that stared back last night.

I transformed last night
from my normal timid self
  to the beast within.

It was a werewolf.
  A monster—somehow, still me.
I am a werewolf.

16

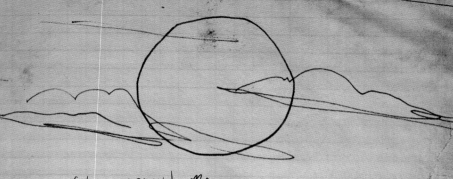

Painful cramps woke me
  and I rolled down off the couch
when I turned last night.

I knew things were bad
 when I could feel skin ripping—
   and could kick down doors.

Out in the backyard,
 I felt my whole body break
under the full moon.

Mailman to werewolf.
 Takes the phrase "going postal"
    to a new level.   17

Unfortunately,
"Man to wolfman" movie scenes...
paintfully dead-on.

Wolf transformation
is as rough as you might guess
but also itchy.

I'll try to describe
werewolf metamorphosis
without throwing up?

oOps →

Changing first tickles,
followed by increased pressure,
and then you puke blood.

18

Your muscles and bones
both rapidly stretch and grow,
but your skin doesn't.

Your skin everywhere—
and yes, I mean everywhere—
is stretched 'till it bursts.

Underneath your flesh,
new growing muscles peek out
and start to sprout hair.

It's around this time,
you realize that your clothes
won't get worn again.

Both your eardrums pop,
then quickly grow back stronger
as your ears sprout up.

All your fingernails
are pushed off of your fingers
by claws underneath.

21

Your large soda gut
goes from a few two-liters
to hairy six-pack.

Your nose, mouth and chin
tear open as a wolf snout
pushes through your face.

Teeth fall to the floor
as new canine incisors
cut your old ones out.

22

It feels like fingers
pushing on both your eyeballs
from inside your skull.

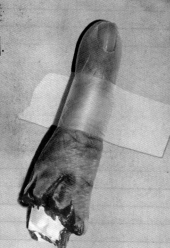

Your eyes don't fall out
but you kind of wish they would
once they start growing.

Your pinky fingers,
as your hands become wolf paws,
shrivel and fall off.

Toenails start to split
as claws pierce out of your toes
and rip through your shoes.

23

That pain in your butt
that feels like constipation
is a tail growing.

smell here

Your new fur is damp
from random moist secretions
and smells like wet dog.

There's throbbing, tearing,
tight nauseating cramping,
and piles of dead skin.

During this process,
the pain is unbearable
and you slip away.

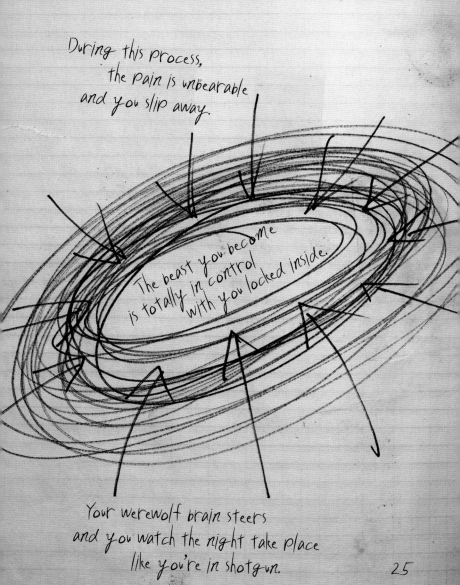

The beast you become
is totally in control
with you locked inside.

Your werewolf brain steers
and you watch the night take place
like you're in shotgun.

25

26

You see yourself change.
You feel yourself get hungry.
You hear yourself howl.

You tear through your house
and watch yourself going wild
out into the night.

You become primal
and all night you act so bad

and it feels so good.

The beast inside you
that you always thought was there
has come out to play.

27

You run from your yard
as a beast into the night,
looking for some fun.

You want to find food,
you want to tear things apart,
and you want your Rose.

Howling at the moon
never makes much sense to you,
but it feels so good.

Now, for some reason,
all you want to do is kill
your next-door neighbors.

The first thing you eat
is a cute little rabbit
who lived in your yard.

The next thing you eat
is a cute little old man
     who lived down the street.

You kill a pet cat
and go straight to Rose's house
     to give her a gift.

Nothing shows true love
     like a pile of dead housecats
left on her front porch.

Everything's a blur
mixed with dirt, hair, pain and blood

until the sunrise.

The next thing you know,
you're normal, naked, outside,
and your stomach's full.

31

When you transform back,
it's not nearly as painful...
you just shrink and shed.

Your nose, ears, eyes, teeth,
pinky fingers, nails and gut
all grow back in place.

You must then decide:
Do you first wash off the blood
or cover your junk?

Your next dilemma
is how to make it back home
without being seen.

32

Once inside your house,
you find your love mix CD
smashed into pieces.

And now here you sit,
with a neighbor-filled stomach,
writing poetry.

...I didn't make it.
Writing those last few haiku

made some puke come up.

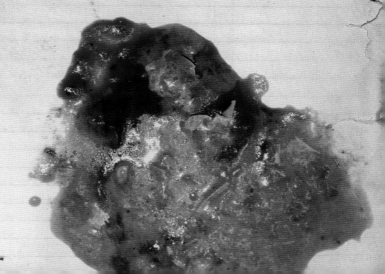

My dog is missing,
but he must have found those bones
and brought them inside.

I've got that all wrong.
Those bones were inside my dog.
I remember now.

When one loves one's pet—
typically, eating that pet
is not considered:

If one can get past
all the desperate barking,
raw dog tastes awesome.

35

His meaty dog thighs
were like eating chicken legs
but with bloody hair.

I'll miss my Lupé,
but with this indigestion,
I might see him soon.

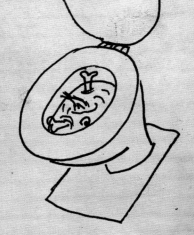

A terrible stench
is seeping out from my pants.
I think it's Shih Tzu.

36

I should call in sick
and do some work on my house
and on my colon.

Don't worry, my friend.
   I will write you again soon,
dear haiku journal.

37

Dear haiku journal,
Are there three full moons a month
or is there just one?

Do werewolves transform
more than just one night a month?
I'll find out tonight.

Not taking chances.
I should drive way out of town
to not hurt people.

Out in the country—
late afternoon, in my car—
wearing a sweatsuit.

Praying clothes don't rip.
Praying not to kill again.
Praying I don't change.

Prayer didn't work
and neither did the sweatsuit.
Now, where did I park?

Naked once again.
Therefore, no keys once again.
Hope the car's unlocked.

A distant farmhouse
with four parked ambulances
brings back memories.

All those EMTs
won't be needing those stretchers.
Maybe some baggies.

41

I find my car locked,
but that's not a big problem
since the windshield's gone.

Naked on the hood,
I climb through the broken glass
and find my car keys.

As I drive back home,
I'm glad I have sunglasses
to help block the wind.

A few cars pass me
as I try to look normal,

windowless and nude.

43

Why is murder wrong?
The more I think about it,
the better it sounds.

That soul inside you—
it's what is inside that counts.
I want your outside.

Souls are eternal
and don't need bodies to live,
so why the upkeep?

Souls go to heaven.
Bodies are just part-time homes.
Let me help you pack.

44

If heaven sounds nice,
I'm doing you a favor.
Have fun. I'm eating.

With all this killing,
it helps to justify it
for guilt-free dining.

Please do not judge me.
It's not my fault I'm this way,
dear haiku journal.

45

Dear haiku journal,
A third full moon is coming.
I need to prepare.

I wait in my house
and sit on my couch naked,
so I don't rip clothes.

46

The werewolf in me
      can't care less about our stuff.
   I keep losing doors.

   I take down the screens
and prop a few doors open
      to better my odds.

      The morning after
         a night of eating people
      can be a bit rough.

   You feel hungover
after a werewolf evening,
      but with more remorse.

47

That guy I ate last,
I need to get out of me
and in a toilet.

When people eat corn
and spot them in their feces—
teeth are that way, too.

The full moon peeks out
above the horizon line.
Here we go again!

Is it terrible
that I am so excited,
dear haiku journal?

Dear haiku journal,
Sorry I haven't written.
It's been a few months.

That werewolf problem
where three days a month I kill...
it's still going strong.

For the past eight weeks,
I have delivered the mail
like my life is fine.

Though mostly normal,
I have werewolf tendencies
that last through the month.

My new unibrow
is not as embarrassing
as my new tongue hair.

My curved fingernails
are perfect for back scratching
but bad for wiping.

51

All of my senses
seem about five times stronger—
which has pros and cons.

I can hear better,
even though both my ear holes
are clogged with whiskers.

Spiders have eight legs,
each of which I hear stomping
on my hardwood floors.

With heightened hearing,
current pop songs hurt my ears
more than they used to.

52

Nothing is blurry.
I no longer need glasses
to find my glasses.

With heightened eyesight,
I watch microscopic bugs
on my eyelashes.

53

My new swinging stride
  speeds mail delivery time—
with my wider steps.

I must remember,
when I'm about to shape shift:
  Wear clothes I don't want.

I now notice scents
seeping from old couch cushions
  as I watch TV.

My new sense of smell
makes for a rough addition,
with my messy house.

Constant gag reflex,
thanks to new strands of long hair
growing in my mouth.

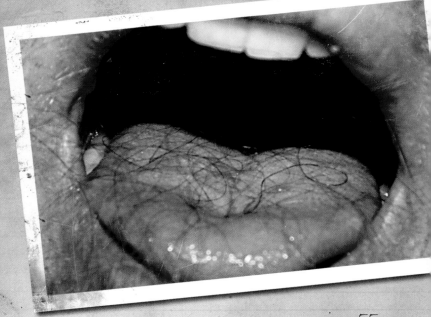

55

I've gained new habits
    that make delivering mail
more complicated.

Strangers seem surprised
    when a distant car alarm
causes me to howl.

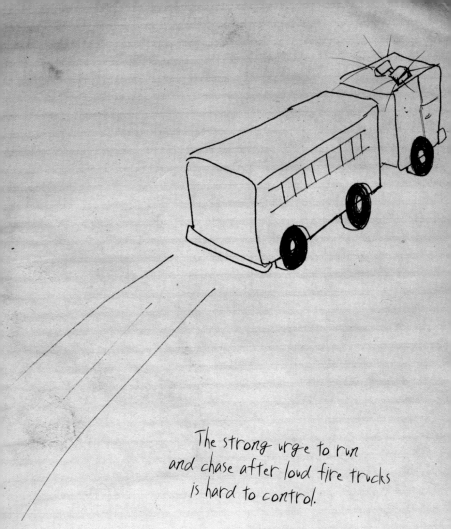

The strong urge to run
and chase after loud fire trucks
is hard to control.

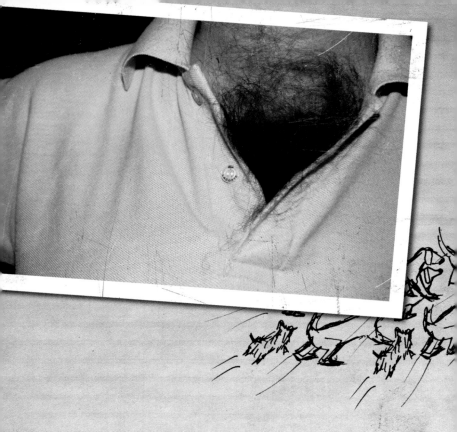

I constantly push
my overgrowing chest hair
back into my shirt.

I walk down the streets
like a pied piper for dogs
who follow behind.

Frequent fantasies
involve Rose rubbing fingers
behind my earlobes.

How can werewolves die?
"Silver bullets through the heart"
seems most consistent.

Should I really dodge
only the silver bullets?
I bet lead hurts, too.

It is hard to check
the type of metal bullet
when it's fired at you.

"Lycan" or "Wolfman"—
it comes down to preference.
I prefer "Werewolf."

Take lycanthropy,
subtract the long teeth and hair:
Cannibalism.

Science might call it
clinical lycanthropy—
with less delusion.

Cannibalism
is a fairly glaring con,
but there are some pros.

That thinning bald patch
that had started to peek through
no longer exists.

61

My head still itches,
weeks after I'm a werewolf,
from leftover ticks.

It's hard to eat food
when my head leans over plates
and bugs jump for it.

A werewolf headache—
my scalp is a battlefield
between ticks and lice.

With so many bugs,
I try not to scratch my scalp
or my hands get wet.

My lice look like salt
and my ticks look like pepper

falling in my lunch.

63

I need a hairbrush
with a much longer handle
to get to my back.

When I comb my head
I usually end up
combing my face, too.

My hairbrush is gross,
filled with knots of hair and twigs
and maybe some veins.

When I take showers,
I tend to use as much Nair
as I do shampoo.

I shave my palms now,
since work friends like to make jokes—
which can turn awkward.

65

24

25

30

31

● Full Moon

JUNE

S	M	T	W	T	F	S
	1	2	3	4	5	6
7	8	9	10	11	12	13
14	15	16	17	18	19	20
21	22	23	24	25	26	27
28	29	30				

AUGUST

S	M	T	W	T	F	S
						1
2	3	4	5	6	7	8
9	10	11	12	13	14	15
16	17	18	19	20	21	22
23	24	25	26	27	28	29
30	31					

The term "moonstrating"
some might find a bit vulgar,

but it is fitting.

One cycle a month,
my hormones get out of whack
and blood is involved.

I get real moody
when it's that time of the month.
I cry more at songs.

I'm the only guy
who has monthly circled dates
on his calendar.

My new life is odd
but it is so much more fun,

dear haiku journal.

Dear haiku journal,
You're not going to believe
what the new me did!

I could never do
what I did this afternoon
before that dog bite.

Should I be nervous
if the werewolf part of me
gives me confidence?

On Rose's front porch,
I stood and knocked on her door.
    Then I asked her out.

69

She said, "Yes!" to me,
and we were both caught off guard
          when I said, "That's right."

Maybe it's just me,
    but when did Rose's pants leg
      become seductive?

Our date was tonight.
I thought it went pretty well.

She might not agree.

71

We went out for steak.
I ordered a rare sirloin.
She got a salad.

As fate would have it,
she's a vegetarian.

I'm the opposite.

Before I was bit,
I had never kissed a girl—
but that changed tonight.

Right around the time
she said she loved animals,
I grabbed her and kissed.

It could have gone worse,
though most kissing fantasies
have less fighting back.

My tongue in her mouth
probably reminded her
of a piece of meat.

She got a taxi
and I drove home by myself,
proud that I made out.

My beautiful Rose:
Know that wherever you run,
I'll be chasing you.

Who I wish I was,
the wolf helps me to become,
dear haiku journal.

75

Dear haiku journal,
A whole bottle of mouthwash
can't kill my cat breath.

Is it raspberry
or blood stains under my nails?
I'll guess raspberry.

Rabies prevention—
once a topic I would mock,
now one I Google.

If you think tacos
are hard for you to digest,
try passing chipmunks.

I wake up at night
with an awkward new desire
to go pee outside.

In conversation,
burping up a severed toe
can make things awkward.

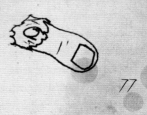

When the moon is full
in the middle of the day—

those days suck for me.

REGISTERED

Werewolves leave claw marks
on trees, cars, et cetera,
because it feels good.

Like a hand massage,
clawing makes small vibrations
that help calm me down.

I can't remember
if wanting to lick people
is something that's new.

Delivering mail
seems like it would go faster
running on all fours.

My job is harder
since now when I see rabbits,
I have to chase them.

79

Eating fat people
is like digesting fast food.

Good now; hurts later.

People in good shape
are like eating fruit smoothies—
with chunks of raw meat.

If you often say,
"His bark is worse than his bite,"
we have yet to meet.

Think my waist will tear
these X X X L sweatpants,
dear haiku journal?

Dear haiku journal,
I have had a ~~rough~~ rough morning,
so pardon these ~~smears~~ smears.

You ever wake up
and find one eye is missing?
That was my morning.

I learned the hard way,
if you're injured as a wolf,
those injuries stay.

Feeling immortal,
I let some girl throw a punch,
and now I'm one-eyed.

My ~~right~~ left eye's last view
was her car keys in her hand
as she punched my face.

I would have stopped her,
had I known that werewolf eyes
would never grow back.

83

I think I won though.
She may have taken my eye,
but I took her hip.

While I can still see,
she is no longer walking—
or living, really.

She went down fighting.
In fact, currently, her hip
is causing heartburn.

My missing eyeball
will be a bit hard to hide
while bringing the mail.

I'm staring for hours,
with a flashlight and mirror,
into my socket.

Though not hygienic,
touching inside my eye hole
is hard to pass up.

It's hard to erase
the urge to fill the socket
with a play-doh ball.

When I close my eye,
is that considered blinking,
or is it winking?

My newest pet peeve
is when my useless eyelid
sticks inside the hole.

Temporary fix:
With a napkin and duct tape,
I cover the hole.

Glass eyeballs online
take six weeks to deliver
and cost a month's pay.

Only costume shops
with large pirate selections
sell eyeball patches.

I bought an eye patch
but had to cover over
the anchor image.

When people question,
I blame LASIK surgery:
"Never use coupons."

My depth perception
makes you seem further away,
dear haiku journal.

Dear haiku journal:
Werewolf movies often lie.
Torn jeans don't stay on.

Despite the movies,
I do not have the desire
to surf on van roofs.

Of all werewolf films,
Teen Wolf's popularity
confuses me most.

After I transform,
the last thing I want to do
is play basketball.

Dear Michael J. Fox,
Hop in your time machine car,
and don't make Teen Wolf.

When I get hungry,
my mind daydreams about meat
and girls in red hoods.

Children's fairy tales
give harmful werewolf advice.

We don't want baskets.

If you don't notice
a werewolf dressed as grandma,
then come here, grandkid.

What big teeth I have.
All the better to tear through
digestive systems.

Why wouldn't the wolf,
once the girl shares her schedule,
shrug and then eat her?

If you're in my woods
wandering to grandma's house,
you won't make it there.

Me, the big bad wolf.
You, little red riding hood.
This will get messy.

93

Those three little pigs
would have been eaten too fast
for a fairy tale.

That ten-page story
should be a five-word sentence:
"A wolf eats three pigs."

If you seek safety
in a house of branch or hay,
you've lived long enough.

You won't let me in?
Well, little pig, little pig,
no more playing nice.

Hide in a brick house?
I would huff and puff at it,
then break a window.

94

It's hard to eat pigs
when their chinny chin chin hair
gets stuck between teeth.

Once the pigs are gone
and the bones lose their flavor...
time for their owner.

I love eating pigs.
Farmers who love eating pigs—
I love eating more.

95

or
ple,
uffi-
ough
that
once
incin-
nk in a

me with
teel, cast
void grills
e of sheet
ease drips,
ently," says
ecting pan,
p, she says.
hen removed.

to the sides so ashes can't slip down. Vents at the top and the bottom, or on either side, of the grill are important for cross ventilation, which moves smoke and heat around the grill ok for a ti

I think about girls
a lot more than I used to.
Hot girls eating meat.

Girls in red raincoats:
Be sure to keep those hoods down.

Quit leading me on.

When I picture girls
with dead chipmunks in their teeth,
my heart could explode.

You know that fifth toe
that you wonder if you need?
Turns out that you don't.

If you lose a toe,
make sure it's the little one.
Big ones are useful.

People can still run
if I just eat little toes.
Big toes, though... they're mine.

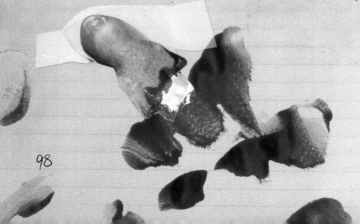

Five o'clock shadow,
even if I shave at noon,
now shows up by two.

I need more razors
and I need new furniture,
dear haiku journal.

Dear haiku journal:
Love makes us do crazy things,
which explains this limp.

Rose won't answer calls,
open the door when I pound,
or keep the dead cats.

Against good judgment,
I visited Rose last night.
It did not go well.

Around 3am,
as if to say, "Come on in,"
her house lights were off.

100

Rose was sound asleep,
which was sweet for me to watch
through her back window.

I don't use doorknobs.
Who knows if her door was locked?
It opened for me.

She didn't answer
when I smashed apart her house,
yelling out her name.

I couldn't find her.
Rose's hospitality
needs a little work.

She was being rude,
as if she didn't recall
I bought her salad.

I picked up her scent,
which led me to her closet
and this bullet wound.

Two bullets pass me—
and considering my size,
I am hard to miss.

Bullet number three
hit the wall like the others...
but went through me first.

103

Rose aimed at my chest,
both her hands holding a gun
that smoked as I fell.

I slid to the floor
as Rose lowered the weapon
that punched through my chest.

Nothing can hurt me
when I'm in my werewolf form.
Excluding bullets.

Rose jumped over me
as if I didn't exist
as I moaned her name.

104

If you shoot a guest
and make a gaping chest wound,
offer an ice pack.

If silver bullets
can instantly kill werewolves,
those must have been lead.

Rose called 911,
which pushed me over the edge
and I let her know.

I slowly stood up,
and as I stared in her eyes,
I flexed and I howled.

An operator
spoke loudly through Rose's phone:
"Having dog trouble?"

I clawed for the phone,
which is why she will have scars
for life on her face.

Rose shot me again,
which is why I have a limp
and only one knee.

I fell to the floor
as Rose screamed about werewolves
and ran out the door.

The smell of her blood
helped me to regain my strength.
But not my kneecap.

I hobbled back up
and limped out through the front door,
chasing after her.

Rose loved to play games,
but I'm the dog on her leash
who will not play dead.

Rose had a good lead
but I was still catching up—
until the cops came.

The police siren
was a song I had to join
and I howled again.

Rose pointed at me
and the police pulled their guns
as I ran away.

I woke up outside,
nude but normal, in a bush
in my own backyard.

My kneecap is gone.
In its place: a crusty scab
peppered with wolf hair.

The hole through my chest
has closed up and is healing,
but it hurts to cough.

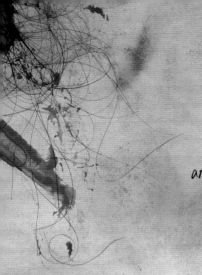

If the bullet hit
any of my main organs,
I guess they heal, too.

I'm taking to bed
my broken chest, knee and heart,
dear haiku journal.

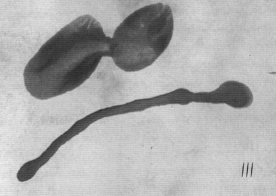

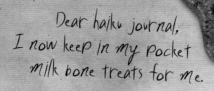

Dear haiku journal,
I now keep in my pocket
milk bone treats for me.

I knew something changed
when my recurring daydreams
included dog bones.

When dogs near my yard,
screaming, "My territory!"
is now a habit.

I now fight the urge
to shove my nose in crotches.
Socially awkward.

Dry dog food is gross,
but that fancy small can stuff
makes my mouth water.

Replacing tuna
with a tin of canned dog food
is great in salads.

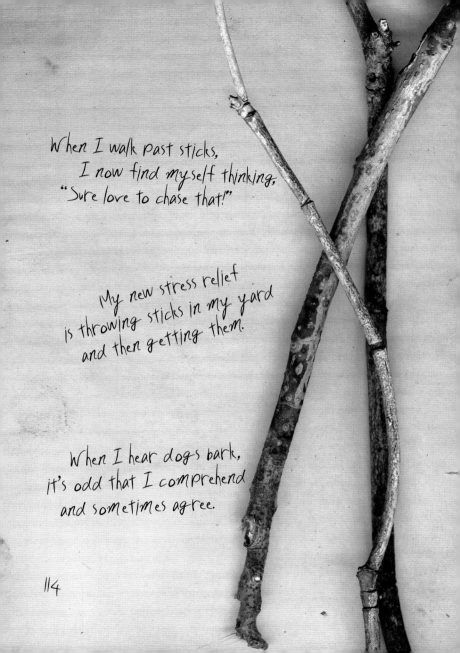

When I walk past sticks,
   I now find myself thinking,
"Sure love to chase that!"

My new stress relief
is throwing sticks in my yard
and then getting them.

When I hear dogs bark,
it's odd that I comprehend
and sometimes agree.

114

Now I understand,
like everlasting pretzels,
why dogs chew on bones.

I need a breath mint.
A smell worse than garlic breath:
my pancreas breath.

Pet stores drive me mad
with all their open cages,
like a salad bar.

115

My heightened senses
help me know where people are.
I'm a good stalker.

Most frown on stalking,
but if it makes you happy...
I say stalk away.

If you like a girl,
follow her all around town
and try to smell her.

People who eat fast
and call it "wolfing down food,"
have no idea.

Raw hamburger meat
is my new favorite snack.
Great in cereal.

Coughing up hairballs
is more like vomiting hair.
Cats do it cuter.

Shape-shifter powers:
You mind working on my gut,
or is that too much?

Blue moon leftovers.
Months with two full moon cycles
make me feel pudgy.

Wearing my wool coat,
I'm a wolf in sheep's clothing—
and fashionable.

118

To ease suffering,
I try to recite poems
as my body breaks.

Allen Ginsberg's "Howl"
was not the best poem choice.
Moloch! This hurts bad!

119

Ever get the urge
to chase, catch, shake and kill moles?
I get that now, too.

Belly button lint
used to just be my shirt fuzz,
and not as scabby.

As I fall asleep,
I dream of fields filled with cats
and big steel-toed boots.

That's me! I'm famous!
the murders are on the news,
dear haiku journal!

Dear haiku journal,
    Love cowers in the corner,
trapped as I close in.

In Rose's mailbox,
I left her a love letter.

FUN PLAYING
LAST NIGHT!

Somehow this letter
made its way to the Police,
who knocked on my door.

They searched my whole house
and asked about the scratched walls.
"I have dog problems."

The cops brought me in
and asked a lot of questions
about me and Rose.

I kind of told lies.
"It wasn't me who chased her..."
...but something in me.

"Tripping down my stairs
led to missing knee and eye.
It was a bad fall."

"You know puppy love—
Rose just wants my attention.
This is how she flirts."

They didn't buy it,
but without hard evidence,
the cops let me go.
They would have had proof
if they took a stool sample
instead of just pee.

As I walked away,
a policeman said to me,
    "Stay away from Rose.

"She knows what you are,
and I think I saw it too,
last night in the road.

"I shot at something
    that looked a lot like a wolf
and a bit like you.

"I've seen the movies
so I made my own bullets
with melted silver.

"I'll be at her house
all night while the moon is up,
looking for trouble."

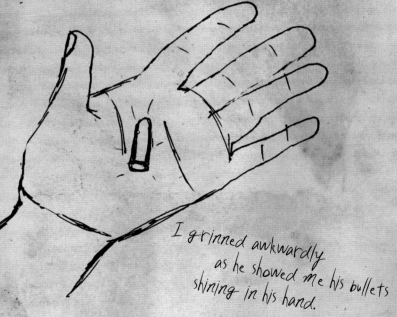

I grinned awkwardly
as he showed me his bullets
shining in his hand.

As I turned to leave,
I said to the policeman,
"Give my love to Rose."

"I need to get home.
I have a big dinner planned.
Eating pig tonight."

I left the station
and made it home just in time.
The moonrise is soon.

Tonight is the night
  I will see my Rose again
and make her my pet.

To love a woman—
and force her to be like you
is the quest of man.

129

Perhaps, just one bite
and she will become like me:
a werewolf in love.

Under the moonlight,
we will both eat together
a slab of raw cop.

He will try to run,
and we will play with our food
by letting him hope.

We'll both tackle him
      into a patch of soft grass
   and have a picnic.

131

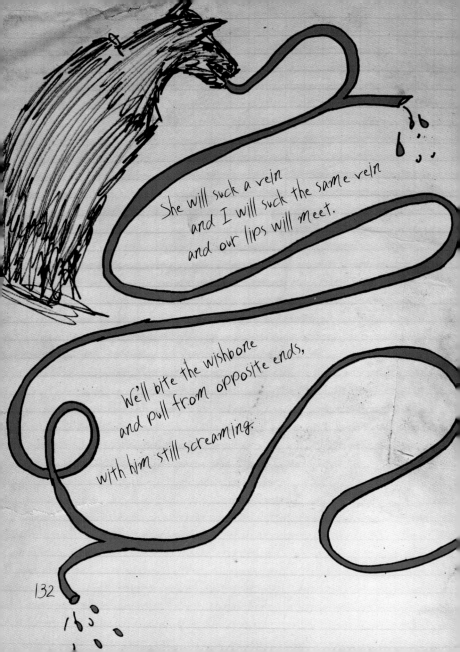

She will suck a vein
and I will suck the same vein
and our lips will meet.

We'll bite the wishbone
and pull from opposite ends,
with him still screaming.

132

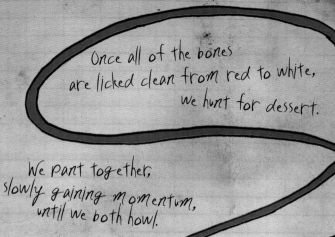

Once all of the bones
are licked clean from red to white,
we hunt for dessert.

We pant together,
slowly gaining momentum,
until we both howl.

Hearing in my head
is howling in harmony
makes my eye water.

133

We leap above fog
and catch a glimpse of the stars,
fading into dawn.

As the sun rises,
we transform back together
in each other's arms.

We then quickly run
through backyards back to my place,
and sleep on my couch.

134

Tonight is the night
(unless I'm reading Rose wrong),
when my dreams come true.

When the moon is full,
open up your throat and howl
and all will feel right.

The werewolf is near.
My whole body is shaking,
or is that my nerves?

135

When I get back home,
I'll tell you all that happened—
unless I get killed.

I will be right back.
Don't you worry about me,
dear haiku journal.

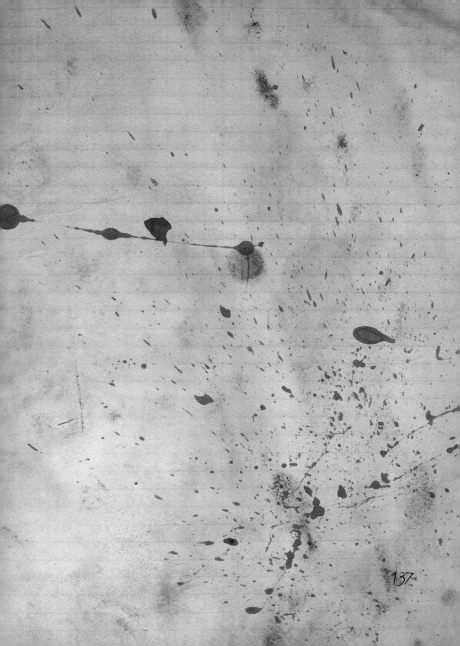

137

curio press

About the Design

Werewolf Haiku is designed by Lisa Kuhn, owner of Curio Press, located in Cincinnati, Ohio. Curio Press is devoted to high quality book design and packaging. For more information, visit: www.curiopress.com

About the Author

Ryan Mecum has loved werewolves since he was ten years old, when he snuck out of bed in the middle of the night and watched Silver Bullet on cable. Werewolf Haiku is the third book of Ryan's Horror Haiku series. He also wrote Zombie Haiku and Vampire Haiku. Ryan graduated from the University of Cincinnati with a degree in English Literature. He lives in Cincinnati, Ohio, with his wife and children. You can find more information about him at www.ryanmecum.com.

Reading these "haiku"
and loving me anyway:
This one's for Missy.